Horrible Histories

SICK!

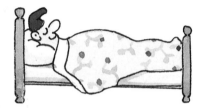

CONTENTS

Watts Books
London • New York • Sydney

THE HUMAN MACHINE

Your body is an amazing machine. It has hundreds of muscles and bones, thousands of kilometres of tubes, millions of nerves and billions of cells. All this is hidden beneath your skin. Unless we know how things work we can't fix them when they go wrong. People used to be very ignorant about how bodies worked. This led to many strange and dangerous treatments. The first real attempts to discover how the body works were made by the ancient Greeks. Since the European Renaissance, and especially in the last three hundred years, medical research has accelerated.

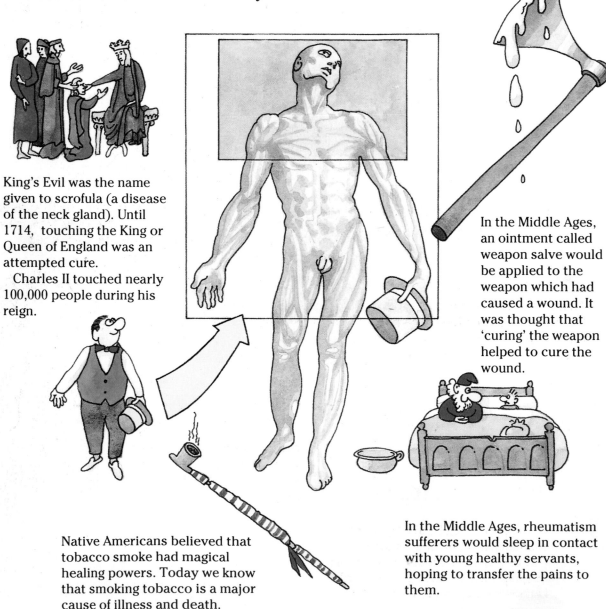

King's Evil was the name given to scrofula (a disease of the neck gland). Until 1714, touching the King or Queen of England was an attempted cure.
  Charles II touched nearly 100,000 people during his reign.

In the Middle Ages, an ointment called weapon salve would be applied to the weapon which had caused a wound. It was thought that 'curing' the weapon helped to cure the wound.

Native Americans believed that tobacco smoke had magical healing powers. Today we know that smoking tobacco is a major cause of illness and death.

In the Middle Ages, rheumatism sufferers would sleep in contact with young healthy servants, hoping to transfer the pains to them.

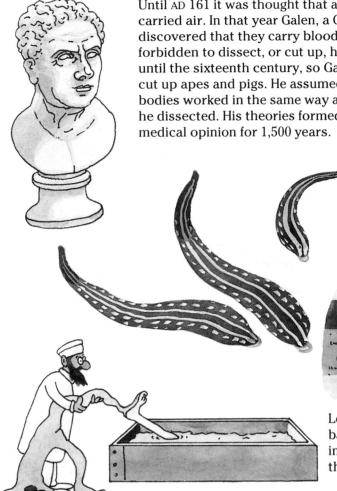

Until AD 161 it was thought that arteries carried air. In that year Galen, a Greek doctor, discovered that they carry blood. It was forbidden to dissect, or cut up, human bodies until the sixteenth century, so Galen used to cut up apes and pigs. He assumed human bodies worked in the same way as the animals he dissected. His theories formed the basis of medical opinion for 1,500 years.

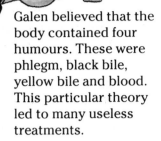

Galen believed that the body contained four humours. These were phlegm, black bile, yellow bile and blood. This particular theory led to many useless treatments.

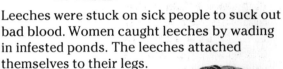

Leeches were stuck on sick people to suck out bad blood. Women caught leeches by wading in infested ponds. The leeches attached themselves to their legs.

All major religions and civilisations at one time or another have banned dissection of the human body. However, ancient Hindus were allowed to soak bodies in water and then peel back the skin so that they could look inside and study them.

Andreas Vesalius, an Italian doctor, wrote the first scientific text on the human body in 1543. He was condemned to death by the Catholic Church, but was saved by the Holy Roman Emperor.

Throughout the Middle Ages, the examination of urine was the main way of diagnosing disease. This was despite the fact that doctors didn't know what they were looking for.

It seems that cleanliness was valued by some ancient civilisations. The remains of public baths 4,500 years old have been found in Pakistan, Iraq and Egypt.

LIVING CONDITIONS

The average lifespan of Stone Age people was less than eighteen years. The main causes of death were disease and violence.

Improvements in farming methods, sanitation, housing and medicine have helped people to live longer and longer, but many of the major diseases of history have been made worse by the crowded living conditions of town life. The importance of cleanliness was not properly understood until the nineteenth century.

By 1900, city dwellers in Europe and the USA could expect to live until fifty. Slum housing, bad water and air pollution meant that people still died younger than today.

In the USA today, both men and women can expect to live to at least seventy. The reason that people live so much longer nowadays is due far more to public health measures and a good diet than to the wonders of modern medicine.

Castles had toilets built into the walls. Toilet waste fell outside the castle.

A toilet built over the River Thames collapsed while occupied. In the Middle Ages, toilets often emptied directly into rivers.

A pomander is a perfumed ball which some people carried to ward off infection and counteract bad smells.

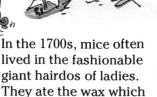

In the 1700s, mice often lived in the fashionable giant hairdos of ladies. They ate the wax which held the hair in place.

Medieval people often used the floor as a toilet. Layers of reeds or rushes were spread on top occasionally. When mixed with clay, the waste made saltpetre, an ingredient of gunpowder. A saltpetre law forbade the paving of floors in England until 1634.

Norman castles were dirty places, but they sometimes had large bathrooms where families could bathe together.

Medieval towns had open-air bath houses called stews. Men and women bathed together.

Puritans didn't approve of bathing. They felt it weakened the body.

In many houses, cellars were used as cess pits, which were shovelled out occasionally into a cart. Water contaminated by cess pits spread typhoid and cholera.

Slipper baths, which took their name from their shape, hid the bather from servants who poured in water. They were popular in nineteenth century America, as can be seen from western movies.

Tuberculosis was spread by spitting and coughing. Spittoons were commonplace in the nineteenth century. These were containers in public places for spitting into.

Two thousand five hundred tonnes of lead from car exhausts are released into the atmosphere every year. Lead limits brain growth in children.

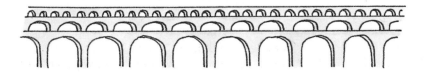

Until the smog laws of 1962, a photochemical smog covered the city of Los Angeles for 212 days of the year.

Modern living conditions can also cause disease. Large office buildings with windows which can't be opened can be breeding grounds for diseases.

In 350 BC, the Romans built the first aqueduct to bring water to Rome. Roman cities had piped clean water and sewers. It took modern European cities until 1800 to match their standards.

YOU ARE WHAT YOU EAT

Variety in the food we eat is important to health. The Romans ate a huge range of foods. Today, the Chinese eat a wider variety of food than any other peoples. Delicacies include snake, fried fish stomachs and chickens' feet.

For most of history human beings have not been farmers, they have been hunter-gatherers. The human body is designed to work best on the sort of food which might be eaten by a hunter-gatherer, such as fresh fruit and nuts with a small amount of meat. Farming is a relatively recent invention, and modern factory food is even more recent.

People only started farming in Europe about 4,000 years ago and modern factory food wasn't produced until 40 years ago. Modern foods are the cause of much ill health; however, the food eaten in the West is much healthier than it has been for several hundred years.

Diatetics is the study of food. It's a very old science. A guide to good eating was written 3,500 years ago in Egypt.

The ancient Greeks thought that food was made of the four elements: earth, air, fire and water. Hot, spicy food was fire. Moist food was water. Dry food was earth. Cool, light food was air.

Children do not grow properly if they eat poor food. Until recently, the Japanese and poorer people in the West were very short because of a bad diet in childhood.

Margarine was one of the first factory foods. Originally it was made of beef fat, milk and minced cow's udders.

Baked dormouse was considered a delicacy by rich Romans.

In the nineteenth century, bread often contained bone dust or chalk, wood shavings and a poisonous chemical called alum to make it look whiter. Mixing bad products with food is called adulteration.

Henry VIII of England suffered from scurvy and other diseases, because he ate hardly anything but meat. Scurvy is a disease caused by not eating enough fresh vegetables.

In the 1800s, an Italian cheese manufacturer sold Parmesan cheese which was mainly made of grated umbrella handles.

COUGHS AND SNEEZES

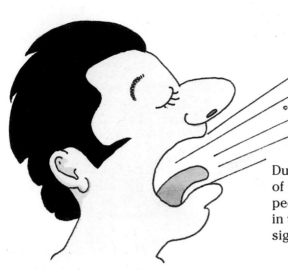

People used to think that disease was caused by evil influences called miasmas. Miasmas were found in things such as wood, soil, water or animals.

During the Spanish flu epidemic of 1918-19, which killed more people than all the soldiers killed in the First World War, huge signs in New York announced:

IT IS UNLAWFUL TO COUGH OR SNEEZE

$500 FINE

Infectious diseases are passed from one person to another. They are caused by tiny life forms called germs.

A sneeze bursts from the nose at 100 mph. It blasts as many as 100,000 drops of germ-rich mucus up to a distance of 2.5 metres away. If the sneezer has a disease, the germs in any of these drops may spread that disease.

The idea that tiny creatures might cause disease was discussed in a Roman encyclopaedia 2,000 years ago, but it could not be proved because germs are far too tiny to see with the naked eye. Zacharias Janssen is thought to have invented the microscope in 1590. By 1677, microscopes had become powerful enough for another Dutchman, Anton Van Leeuwenhoek, to discover single-celled 'animalcules', or germs.

Typhus was known as gaol fever, where it killed thousands. It was caused by a body louse which could jump from one prisoner to another in crowded prison conditions. This disease also wiped out most of Napoleon's Grande Armée in 1812.

In America, 60 million schooldays are lost each year because of the common cold.

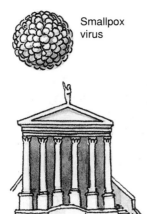
Smallpox virus

Some very small germs called viruses cause diseases. They are so small that they cannot be seen under a standard microscope. Mumps, measles, chicken pox, influenza and the common cold are all caused by viruses.

Louis Pasteur

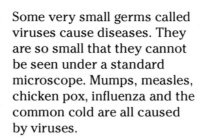

Influenza was recorded in ancient Rome in 412 BC.

Louis Pasteur (1822-95) showed experimentally that infectious diseases are caused by germs. We still use 'pasteurisation', the gentle heating of drinks and foodstuffs, to help prevent infections.

Humans can catch some diseases from animals such as rabies from dogs and fevers from parrots and rabbits.

So many people were killed by cholera in Lower Bengal that the disease was worshipped as the Goddess Cholera.

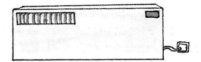

Legionnaires disease was discovered in 1976. It is caused by bacteria that like to live in air conditioning systems in buildings.

Along with many other diseases, leprosy and smallpox were brought back to Europe by eleventh century crusaders.

European colonists spread many infectious diseases around the world. Millions of Native Americans died of smallpox and measles which were unknown in ancient America before the settlers arrived.

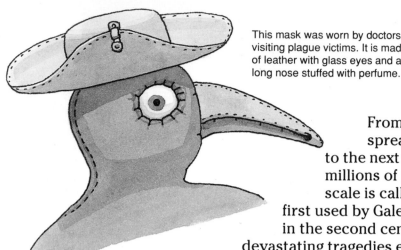

This mask was worn by doctors visiting plague victims. It is made of leather with glass eyes and a long nose stuffed with perfume.

PLAGUE

From time to time a disease will spread rapidly from one person to the next like a forest fire. Sometimes millions of people die. A disease on this scale is called a plague. The word was first used by Galen, the famous Greek doctor, in the second century AD. One of the most devastating tragedies ever was the bubonic plague, otherwise known as the Black Death. It spread from China in the 1330s and killed around 75 million people, 25 million of them in Europe. So many people died that eventually the dead were left to rot where they fell. Bubonic plague continued to haunt Europe for the next two hundred years.

Today, plagues are more often called epidemics. The worst epidemic of modern times was the Spanish flu of 1918-19. It killed 21,600,000 people in 120 days.

During the Black Death in fourteenth century Byzantium, the dead were piled in the towers of the city walls. The stench was horrible.

In 1347, the Mongol army catapulted plague victims into the besieged city of Caffa to infect the inhabitants.

Many Europeans believed that Jews caused the plague by poisoning wells. In Mainz, Germany, 12,000 Jews were burned because of this.

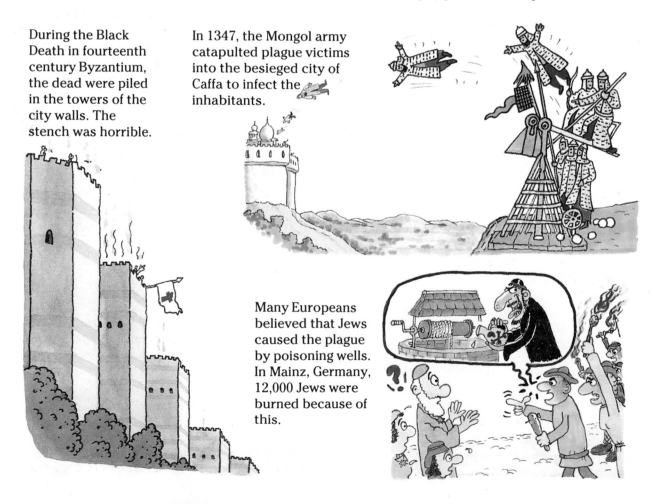

How to tell if you have caught the plague

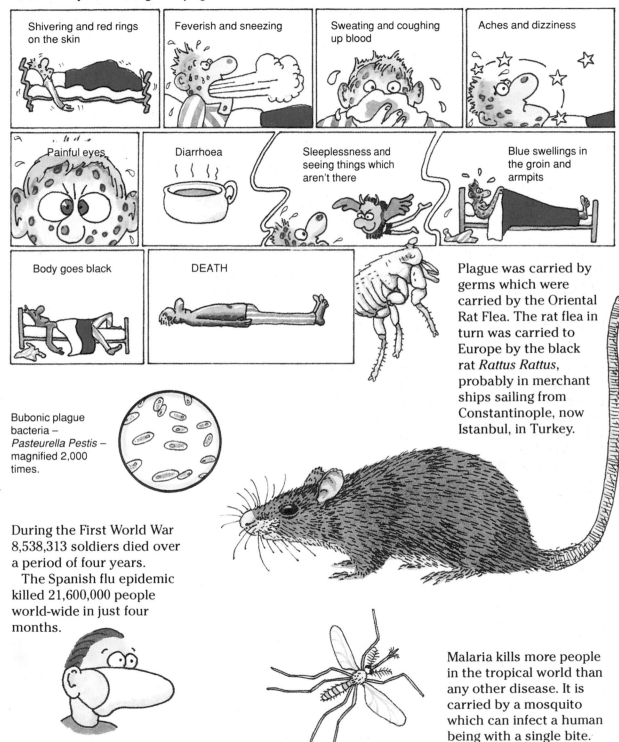

Shivering and red rings on the skin

Feverish and sneezing

Sweating and coughing up blood

Aches and dizziness

Painful eyes

Diarrhoea

Sleeplessness and seeing things which aren't there

Blue swellings in the groin and armpits

Body goes black

DEATH

Plague was carried by germs which were carried by the Oriental Rat Flea. The rat flea in turn was carried to Europe by the black rat *Rattus Rattus*, probably in merchant ships sailing from Constantinople, now Istanbul, in Turkey.

Bubonic plague bacteria – *Pasteurella Pestis* – magnified 2,000 times.

During the First World War 8,538,313 soldiers died over a period of four years.

The Spanish flu epidemic killed 21,600,000 people world-wide in just four months.

During the Spanish flu epidemic, the people of San Francisco could be jailed for not wearing white cotton face masks on the street.

Malaria kills more people in the tropical world than any other disease. It is carried by a mosquito which can infect a human being with a single bite.

Today, a disease called AIDS is spreading rapidly. AIDS is turning into a modern epidemic.

11

DOCTORS AND MEDICINE MEN

Early healers were often magicians or priests. Magical treatments are normal among primitive tribes even today.

Professional doctors are as old as civilisation. The ancient Chinese practised acupuncture 6,000 years ago. Ancient Hindu doctors wrote down their theories in the *Rig Veda* 3,500 years ago. And the ancient Egyptians had doctors, although they were reluctant to treat patients, because if the patient died the doctor was executed.

Western medicine started with the ancient Greeks. Modern doctors still swear the 'Hippocratic oath', named after a Greek doctor called Hippocrates who was born in 460 BC. This oath pledges doctors to maintain the well-being of their patients above all things. Since ancient Egyptian times, doctors have tried to control who can and who can't treat patients. Today, people without medical training are not allowed to call themselves doctors of medicine. This protects the public from ignorant, unqualified doctors.

There were women students at the very first medical school at Salerno in the fourth century AD.

Midwives help women give birth to babies. Male midwives were forbidden to look at their female patients under the bed clothes. So they believed a lady in Godalming when she claimed to have given birth to fifteen rabbits in 1726.

Asclepius was the Greek god of healing.

Eye doctor

Mouth doctor

Ear doctor

Foot doctor

Specialists are nothing new. In ancient Egypt, priest doctors specialised in just one part of the body.

Doctors have been called many rude names in the past such as Sawbones, Leech, Charlatan and Quack. Quack doctors used to tour the Wild West. The name 'quack' comes from the sound they made when shouting to sell their cures. They worked from wagons so that they could make a quick escape if they were discovered to be frauds. Dr Perkins was a famous American quack. His electro-magnetic rods were supposed to draw diseases from the body.

Native American priest doctors, sometimes called Medicine Men, wore a necklace called a soul catcher. They believed that sick people had lost their souls and the necklace helped to capture the soul and return it to the body.

Among the Cree tribe of Native Americans, medicine women cured the sick. Some African tribes have medicine women to this day.

In some developing countries today, men and women are taught basic medical skills so that they can look after poor people in the countryside cheaply. They are nicknamed 'barefoot doctors'.

The Countess of Kent's powder was a quack cure meant to cure the Plague. It contained the feet of large sea crabs, pearls, coral and vipers.

Since the eighteenth century medical schools have turned out more and more doctors each year. Today, there are 465,000 doctors in the USA alone.

TOOLS OF MEDICINE

By using a laser, a modern surgeon can operate inside the body without cutting the skin. If the surgeon wants to look inside a brain he can do so with the huge four-tonne nuclear magnetic resonance scanner.

Today's doctors make use of tools which would have been unimaginable to earlier generations.

But despite the advances in medical technology, some surgical tools have changed very little over the last three thousand years. Knives and saws for cutting flesh and bone are still in use today.

Before the danger of infection was understood, surgeon's saws and knives were often thick with blood and pus from earlier operations.

Today, surgical maggots can be used to clean wounds. They eat the dirt round the wound. Simon Stylites, a hermit who lived on top of a pillar, encouraged maggots to live on his rotting body, saying to them, 'Eat what the Lord has provided.'

Stone Age surgeons often cut holes in the skull with a flint chisel, possibly to stop headaches or to let out devils. This operation is called trepanning. Sometimes boiling oil was poured into the wound.

I don't think much of this new doctor!

It's quite safe!

Early Greek medical tweezers

Some old-fashioned enemal syringes were like huge garden pumps. They squirted liquid up the patient's bottom.

The hypodermic syringe was developed after an Irishman called Francis Rynd invented the hollow needle. The first useful metal syringe was invented in 1853 by a Frenchman called Dr Charles Pravaz. The hypodermic syringe may soon be replaced by a new invention called iontophoresis. This allows injecting without puncturing the skin.

Radioactive chemicals can be injected into the blood stream. Radiation detectors follow their course through the body. This technique can be useful for discovering heart and brain defects.

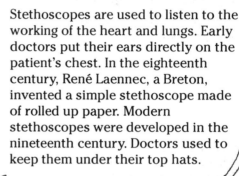

Galileo invented a thermometer in 1593, but it was inaccurate. In the seventeenth century, Robert Boyle made a sealed thermometer which could measure the blood heat of humans.

Stethoscopes are used to listen to the working of the heart and lungs. Early doctors put their ears directly on the patient's chest. In the eighteenth century, René Laennec, a Breton, invented a simple stethoscope made of rolled up paper. Modern stethoscopes were developed in the nineteenth century. Doctors used to keep them under their top hats.

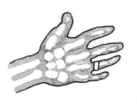

An excess of blood was thought to cause illness. Barber surgeons used a knife, a cup and a piece of string to remove it. The barber's pole symbolises this ancient bloodletting practice.

X-rays were discovered by a German called Wilhelm Roentgen. He used his wife's hand for the first pictures.

Modern X-ray scanner

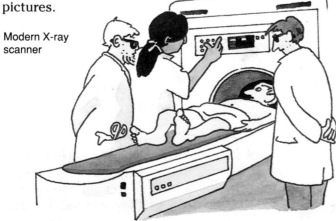

Another method of bloodletting was called cupping. The patient's skin was scratched and the scratch was covered by a hot glass cup. A vacuum formed and blood was sucked into the cup.

ILLS AND PILLS

There are 600,000 plant species in the world. Almost 1,000 useful drugs have been found in them, and only 30,000 species have been studied so far. Most plant species are found in the rain forests which are being cut down at an alarming rate. Chinese pharmacists use many plant medicines unknown in the West.

Swallowing live frogs was thought to ease a sore throat. The slime on the frog's back was thought to be soothing.

A cure for headache was to chew the leaves of the white willow tree. There is a drug in the leaves called willow-herb. A similar drug called aspirin is now being made artificially.

Most drugs come from plants. Until the 1900s people normally ate the whole plant, or parts of it. It was not known how to remove active drugs from plants. Drugs and medicines were prepared by apothecaries or pharmacists in their shops and there were very few drug companies.

Today, drugs can be removed from plants and made into medicine. In the USA alone, over one thousand drug companies manufacture these medicines. Around the world huge sums of money are spent on drugs each year.

The foxglove plant was used in many country remedies. William Withering discovered that it contained a drug called digitalis, which is now used to treat heart conditions.

Curare is used by South American Indians on the tips of their poison darts. It is now used as a muscle relaxant before surgical operations.

Ancient Peruvians chewed the bark of the Cinchona tree to treat mosquito bites. The active drug in the bark is called quinine. It has been used to treat malaria in Europe since 1640.

How pills are made

Some medicines are natural plant extracts, but most are made in factories.

Medicinal powder is poured into a stamping machine.

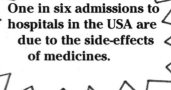

One in six admissions to hospitals in the USA are due to the side-effects of medicines.

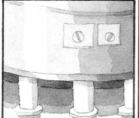

The machine stamps the powder into pill form.

Another machine covers the pills with a protective coating.

The pills then go to the bottling machine.

To stop internal bleeding a bag with a dried toad inside was hung round the neck.

Saliva is a natural medicine. In the wars with ancient Rome, the wives of German warriors used to clean the wounds of their husbands by licking them.

Crushed beetles and pig fat were taken to cure skin rashes.

Alexander Fleming

Penicillin cures many types of infection. It was the first antibiotic to be discovered and is the most useful drug of all time. It comes from a mould which was discovered by accident by Alexander Fleming in 1928.

A fourteenth century cure for the common cold was to boil red onion and mustard together and then stuff the mixture up the sufferer's nose.

Some plants which are commonly consumed today were once thought to be medicines. These include rhubarb, tobacco, tea and coffee.

OPERATIONS

The history of operations is largely one of horrific pain, fear, infection and death. It is less than a hundred years since surgery started to become the fairly safe and painless thing it is today.

Until recently, the only anaesthetics were opium, a drink of alcohol or a blow to the head. There was no knowledge of hygiene, and surgeons would operate in old robes which were soaked in blood and pus from previous operations. Most patients died from shock and pain, from blood loss or from infections.

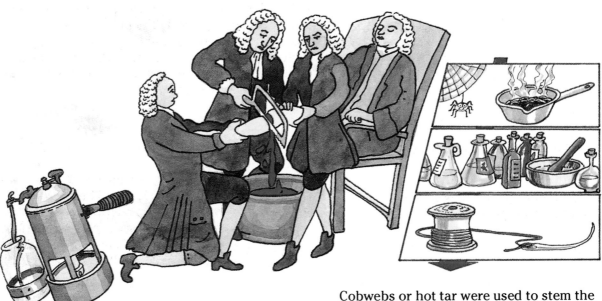

Joseph Lister (1827-1912) developed a method of spraying the area of an operation with carbolic acid. This greatly reduced infections.

Cobwebs or hot tar were used to stem the flow of blood after an operation. Ambroise Paré (1517-1590), who is known as the father of modern surgery, was a French army doctor who treated wounds with ointment instead of hot tar. Today, wounds are stitched up with surgical thread.

Ether, a form of alcohol, became a common anaesthetic in the nineteenth century. The first anaesthetic machine was an ether inhaler used in Boston, Massachusetts, in 1847.

Chloroform was first tested by a party of doctors in 1847. It became the most popular anaesthetic, and was later used on Queen Victoria.

It was very important to perform operations quickly because of the pain and the loss of blood. In the 1840s Robert Lister held the world record for amputating a leg in just two and half minutes.

Modern 'keyhole surgery' allows surgeons to operate without cutting big holes. The surgeon operates through small openings made in the skin, using tiny surgical instruments on flexible rods. Optic fibres connected to a visual display unit allow the surgeon to see what's happening inside the body.

Julius Caesar, the first Roman Emperor, was cut from his mother's body at birth in an operation which is now called a Caesarian section.

Nowadays, surgeons and nurses wear very clean clothes. They also wear masks to stop microbes in their breath entering the patient. The first sterile rubber gloves were developed by the American William Halstead.

Early anaesthetics included alcoholic drinks, opium and other drugs.

The ancient Chinese knew how to stop pain using tiny spikes called acupuncture needles. The technique is still useful today.

This doesn't hurt does it?

No Mum!

Native American culture refused to recognise that pain existed. Children were taught to withstand pain.

SSSS!

Hah hah! Hoo! Don't bother with the operation Doc, I only came here for the gas!

In 1844, an American dentist called Horace Wells used laughing gas to anaesthetise his patients.

ARTIFICIAL PARTS

Artificial parts for the human body have been used for thousands of years. An ancient Chinese document dating from 2000 BC described how artificial legs made from yak bone could be fitted to soldiers.

In addition to their skill in producing artificial parts, modern doctors are able to transplant organs from other people's bodies or even from animals.

Advances in medical science mean that almost any part of the body can now be replaced.

Replacements for hips were first developed in the 1950s.

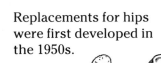

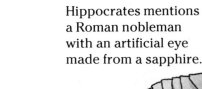

Artificial toes are commonly fitted to victims of frostbite.

Hippocrates mentions a Roman nobleman with an artificial eye made from a sapphire.

A Byzantine general was fitted with a silver nose.

In the sixteenth century, Dr Ambroise Paré designed an artificial arm. It had ratchets and springs so that the elbow could bend and the fingers could open and close.

Artificial pacemakers help the heart to beat regularly. The pacemaker is fitted under the skin and connected to the heart by electronic wires. Batteries are changed every two years. When someone dies, the pacemaker must be removed before cremation or it may explode.

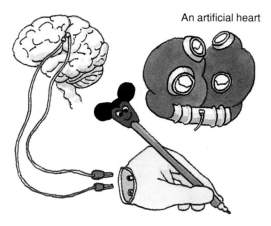

An artificial heart

In the eighteenth century some French scientists attempted to transplant the heart of a sheep.

Using biotechnology, artificial parts can be directly linked to the body nerves so that the artificial part can be operated by the brain.

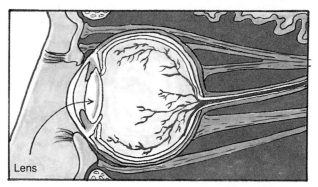

Lens

Cataracts are a clouding of the lens of the eye. The ancient Hindus were removing cataracts 4,000 years ago. Today the lens can be removed and replaced with a contact lens.

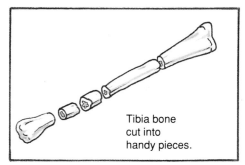

Tibia bone cut into handy pieces.

Bone banks store bone for use in operations. Bones are often cut into small chips for easy storing.

This patient has a burnt bottom!

Hmm! That makes things awkward!

The first eye bank was started in New York in 1944. Eyes can only be stored for a short time before they become useless for surgery. Speed is essential.

At Harvard University in 1984, two burn victims were given skin grafts. The skin had been grown in the laboratory 'skin farm' from tiny pieces. One square centimetre grew to half a square metre. Skin for transplants is often taken from the victim's bottom.

HOSPITALS

In the nineteenth century, operations such as leg amputations took place on the wards. The patients in the beds on either side tried to sleep through the terrifying screams and spurting blood.

Sick people coming into hospital bring infections with them. As many as ten per cent of patients receive an infection while they are in hospital.

Early purpose-built hospitals were dirty and overcrowded. The nurses were often drunk. For most of history, hospitals have been dangerous places to be in. This started to change at the end of the nineteenth century.

The word 'hospital' comes from the Latin word *hospitalis* meaning 'a place for guests'. The idea of a hospital as we understand it today dates from AD 331 when Constantine, the first Christian Roman Emperor, abolished earlier pagan treatment centres.

From the early days of Christianity, Christians were concerned with healing. Phoebe, a Roman noblewoman and friend of Saint Paul, turned her house into a hospital.

As early as 4000 BC there were Greek temples of healing in what is now Turkey. They were dedicated to gods such as Asclepius or Saturn.

Entrance to Monte Casino, Europe's oldest monastic infirmary.

The oldest working hospital in the world is the Hôtel Dieu in Paris. It was founded in AD 600.

In the eighteenth century, the biggest cockroaches in England were said to be at St. Thomas' Hospital. They fed on blood and skin.

Florence Nightingale reformed the nursing profession in the nineteenth century. She insisted that nurses should be clean and wear uniforms. Her reforms began while she was treating British soldiers wounded in the Crimean War. Soon her influence spread round the world. In 1873, two nursing schools following Nightingale's principles were opened in New York.

'Hospice' originally meant a refuge for travellers provided by a monastery. The dogs of the hospice of Great Saint Bernard are famous for finding people lost in the snowy Alps.

Originally, nuns, or sisters, used to tend to the sick. That's why senior nurses in hospitals are known as 'sisters' today.

The Arabs established major hospitals in Baghdad and Cordoba in the ninth century. At that time, Arabic medical knowledge was in advance of Europe.

OPEN WIDE!

Dentistry is the branch of medicine concerned with the teeth and gums. For many centuries, dentistry in Europe was carried out by barbers and barber surgeons, or by travelling healers.

Only in the sixteenth century did dentistry start to become a separate speciality. By 1622, dental surgery was a recognised profession in France.

Dentists were active in the USA by 1800. This was probably because the teeth of the colonists were considered the worst in the world. The founding of the first dental schools in the USA helped establish America as the world's leading centre of dental science.

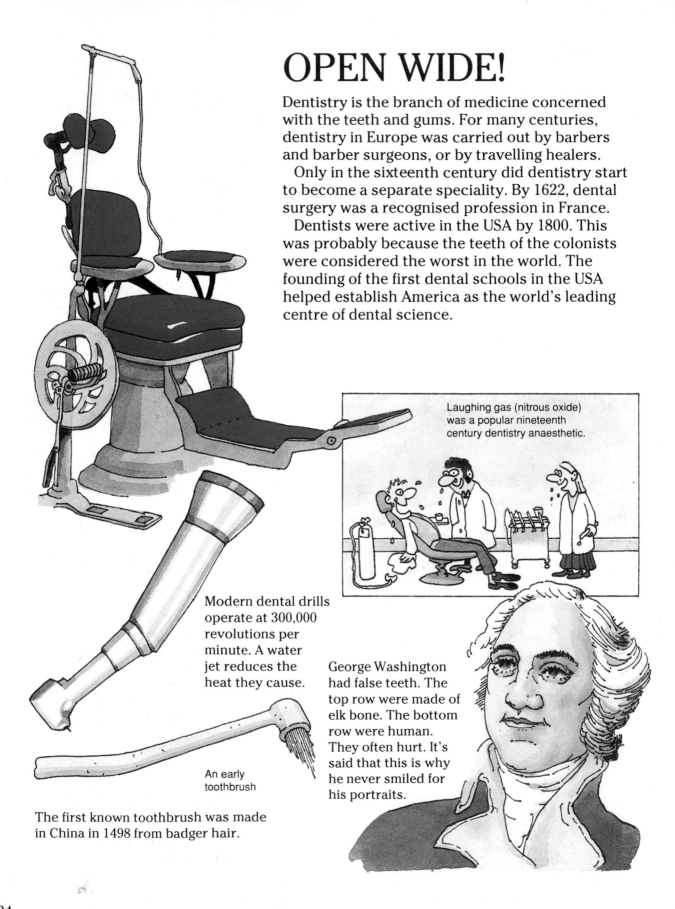

Laughing gas (nitrous oxide) was a popular nineteenth century dentistry anaesthetic.

Modern dental drills operate at 300,000 revolutions per minute. A water jet reduces the heat they cause.

An early toothbrush

George Washington had false teeth. The top row were made of elk bone. The bottom row were human. They often hurt. It's said that this is why he never smiled for his portraits.

The first known toothbrush was made in China in 1498 from badger hair.

Bad teeth and sweets

Sweet foods cause tooth decay. This was first observed by the ancient Greeks.

The Romans ate very little sugar. When the bodies of the victims of the eruption of Vesuvius were uncovered, they were found to have almost perfect teeth.

Elizabeth I of England had jet black teeth caused by tooth decay. Many Elizabethans had rotten teeth and bad breath. They loved marzipan.

Modern Western diet is rich in sugar. Twenty-nine million Americans over twenty years old have no natural teeth of their own. One third of all Americans over thirty-five need dentures.

From clay tablets dated around 3500 BC we know that the ancient Sumerians believed that toothache was caused by tiny worms which gnawed the teeth.

Ancient Etruscan dental bridge

False teeth have been used for thousands of years. Ivory, bone and even wood were used to make them.

Teeth from soldiers killed at the Battle of Waterloo were removed and made into false teeth for other people's mouths.

Scurvy caused by the lack of fresh vegetables or fruit was common among sailors. It causes teeth to fall out and gums to rot.

LOOKING AND FEELING GOOD

Ideas differ on what a healthy person should look like. For instance, in some cultures fatness is admired; in others it is despised. Fat women are admired in Africa and the Middle East. Among several African tribes young women eat special diets to fatten themselves up. Throughout history the people of many cultures have suffered extreme and often bizarre treatments in pursuit of beauty.

Mineral water has been considered healthy since the time of the Romans. In the eighteenth century, whole towns began to grow up around springs of mineral water. In the nineteenth century, long holidays in pure air became popular among the rich. Sanatoriums were built in mountains and other clean, cool, remote places to help treat tuberculosis. Today we have fitness centres and health farms.

From ancient times the Hindus have treated bathing, skin care, teeth cleaning and eye washes as religious necessities. It is said that some Hindu yogis can even pull out their intestines and clean them.

The ancient Greeks loved physical beauty. There were physical education programmes in Greece by 700 BC. All Greek boys were taught to fight and run. But by AD 400 and until AD 1500 most sport was thought sinful in Europe.

Native Americans along the coast of Oregon practised 'head flattening'. Babies' heads were tied to a cradle board so that the skull grew flat. Curiously, the Flathead tribe never did this.

In 1882, false eyelashes that had to be sewn on to the eyelids were advertised for sale in parts of the United States.

In Imperial China the feet of small girls were bound tightly so that the growth of their feet was restricted. This produced the tiny 'lily foot' which was thought attractive. Unfortunately, the girls were crippled for life.

Spas are towns which have grown up around a source of natural mineral water. They are called spas after the town of Spa in Belgium, which was a very popular source of mineral water. The town of Bath was the most fashionable of the English spas. In the nineteenth century at Bath people bathed in the waters fully clothed.

Some African and South American tribes will not allow young men to marry unless they have contracted malaria.

Bath
early nineteenth century

In the Middle Ages, European children were thought to be unhealthy if they did not have any mild symptoms of eczema, a skin disease.

What a healthy looking little boy!

The Padaung women of Burma stretch their necks up to 40 cm long by wearing an increasing number of brass rings. The neck bones become dislocated and eventually the neck is too weak to support the head without the help of the rings.

Cosmetic surgery

I think you've overdone the facelift doctor!

Hmm!

Rhytidectomy - standard facelift
The surgeon cuts the skin beyond the hairline, and pulls the facial skin tightly over the temples and towards the ears. The stretched skin is sewn into place and the excess skin is snipped off.

Woops! This machine's a bit strong!

AARGH!

Liposuction
Liposuction is a technique for sucking fat from the neck, thighs and ankles. A blunt hollow tool called a probelike or a cannula is pushed into the fat through a small cut in the skin. It is attached to a mechanical suction machine and works like a vacuum cleaner.

But I said, 'Just the bottom rib', nurse!

Rib removal
The bottom rib can be removed to make the waist narrower.

PREVENTIVE MEDICINE

Preventive medicine means trying to stay healthy and not to get sick. This can be easier and cheaper than treating people after they have become sick. Preventive medicine involves health education and mass treatments such as vaccination for polio. It may also involve major public works such as new sewerage systems or fresh water supplies. Since Edward Jenner discovered the principle of vaccination in 1796, this has become the most successful of all preventive medicines. By 1980, the World Health Organisation had declared that their vaccination campaign had eradicated smallpox.

In the 1660s the boys of Eton School were punished if they did not smoke tobacco. It was thought that the smoke would protect them from the Great Plague. Today we know that tobacco smoke is not a preventive medicine; in fact it's very dangerous. Half of all long-term smokers die from diseases caused by smoking.

Some early preventive medicines

This doesn't taste like a carrot!

Eat carrots to prevent night blindness.

Just making sure!

Wear a hat during a full moon to prevent madness.

Mum! It's made it worse!

Drink powdered eggshells in milk to prevent bedwetting.

Goodness! What a big nit!

In Britain, 'nit nurses' used to travel round schools. They inspected children's heads for small insects called nits.

Hello! What's your name?

AH CHOO!

Hello Mr Choo!

In the Far East, many people wear a face mask if they have a cold. This is to stop them giving their germs to others.

The spread of diseases can sometimes be prevented if infected people are isolated. This is called quarantining. 'Quarantine' comes from an Italian word meaning forty. Ships suspected of carrying a disease had to wait forty days before being allowed to enter an Italian port. Travellers had to wait forty days outside medieval Italian towns before being allowed to enter.

Nowadays in the West there is so much food that many people eat too much of it. Too much salt can cause high blood pressure which can lead to heart attacks. Education about healthy eating helps people to live longer.

Campaigns to stop people smoking are an important part of modern health education. The following organs which had been damaged by smoking were removed in Australia in 1986:

68   wombs

148   gullets

85   bladders

201   other parts

115   kidneys

82   stomachs

71   tongues

521   lungs

221   voice boxes

Many types of cancer can be cured, if they are detected early enough, by using small doses of nuclear radiation. Cancer screening programs ensure that people at risk visit a clinic regularly, even if they are feeling well.

Regular exercise prevents many illnesses. Nowadays, public education programmes encourage people to take exercise.

Visits to the doctor may become a thing of the past. Already heart monitors can transfer details of a beating heart down a telephone line to a hospital computer. Soon patients may be able to tell all their complaints to computers which will then decide on treatments and dispense medicines.

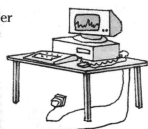

THE FUTURE

On average, people in the developed world live twice as long today as they did a hundred years ago. This is partly due to advancing medical techniques. Scientists are now trying to prevent the aging process.

Meanwhile, in the developing world, millions die young from diseases which are caused by poverty, ignorance and a lack of food and medicines.

Tiny bioelectronic devices can stimulate nerve cells. They enable the brain to operate artificial parts directly. Perhaps bioelectronics are the first step towards replacing the brain entirely.

People with speech defects may be able to speak through electronic voice boxes connected directly to the speech centres of the brain.

Blind people may be able to see through television cameras implanted in their eyes and connected directly to the brain.

Every cell of the body contains DNA molecules. These molecules control who we are and how we grow. Scientists can alter DNA molecules by genetic engineering. In the future, it may be possible to create 'designer people' who will be physically perfect. But what will happen to the rest of us?

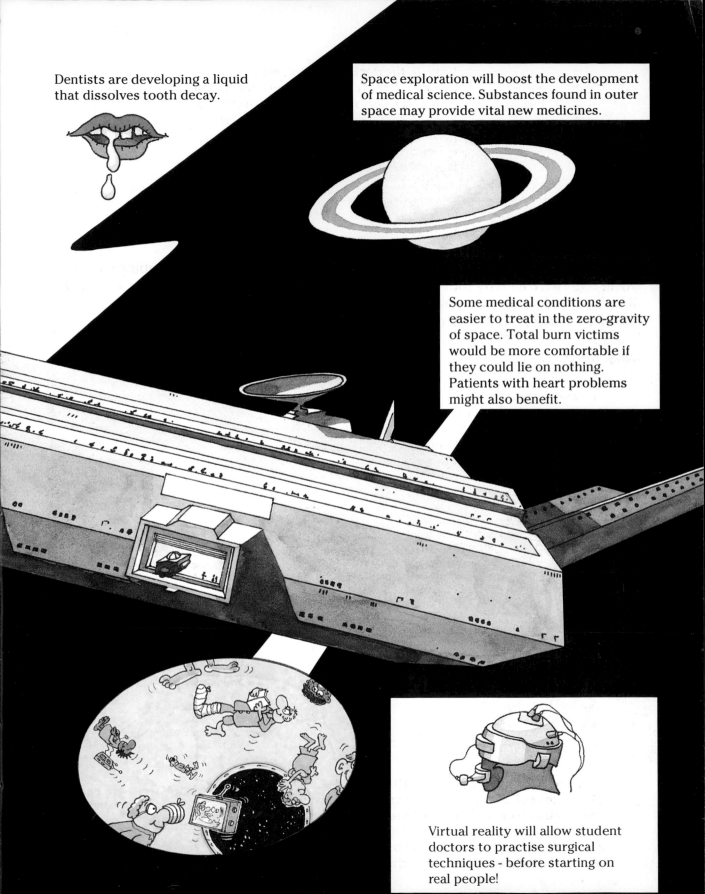

Dentists are developing a liquid that dissolves tooth decay.

Space exploration will boost the development of medical science. Substances found in outer space may provide vital new medicines.

Some medical conditions are easier to treat in the zero-gravity of space. Total burn victims would be more comfortable if they could lie on nothing. Patients with heart problems might also benefit.

Virtual reality will allow student doctors to practise surgical techniques - before starting on real people!

INDEX

First published in 1993 by
Watts Books
96 Leonard Street
London EC2A 4RH

Paperback edition 1994

10 9 8 7 6 5 4 3 2 1

Franklin Watts Australia
14 Mars Road
Lane Cove
NSW 2060

© 1993 Lazy Summer Books Ltd
Illustrated by Lazy Summer Books Ltd

UK ISBN 0 7496 1184 7 (hardback)
UK ISBN 0 7496 1595 8 (paperback)

A CIP catalogue record for this book is
available from the British Library
Dewey Decimal Classification: 610.9

Printed in Belgium

PRINTED IN BELGIUM BY
proost
INTERNATIONAL BOOK PRODUCTION